This Wedding Planner & Organizer Book Belongs to:

_____ and _____

If lost, please contact:

_____

Phone number/Email

Every love story is beautiful, but ours is my favorite.

Future

Mrs & Mrs

Wedding Date:

How To Get The Most Out Of this Wedding Planner & Organizer

There is no particular order that you have to use this book, although you may want to start with the "Pre-Planning Stage" pages to get your ideas started.

We suggest that you flip through all the pages of the book now, so that you know what it contains so that you can refer to the required pages when the time comes.

Use this book:

- To record your research on ceremony & reception venues, florists, caterers, photographers, & much more!
- To keep detailed track of your wedding & honeymoon expenses, including balances still owing on services.
- To use the checklists so you don't forget to do anything, starting 12-15 months before the wedding and all the way to the day of your wedding.
- To create your guest list (up to 400 people).
- To design your seating chart for your guests (up to 400 people).
- To plan your bachelorette parties & bridal showers.
- To pack for your honeymoon (packing list included)
- & more!

HOT TIP: Included in this planner are full pages of tips for choosing your florist, venues, caterers, photographers, & videographers, etc.

Most importantly, have fun as you use this book!

Pre-Planning Stage

BRAINSTORMING THEME FOR WEDDING + COLORS:

VENUE IDEAS:

WEDDING CAKE DESIGN IDEAS:

CHOICE OF MUSIC FOR OUR CEREMONY, FOR OUR FIRST DANCE, FATHER-DAUGHTER DANCE, SPECIAL REQUESTS ETC.

YOU'RE ENGAGED! CONGRATULATIONS! USE THIS PAGE TO GET YOUR CREATIVE THOUGHTS FLOWING. HAVE FUN!

Pre-Planning, continued

IDEAS OF FOOD/MENU:

FLOWER CHOICES:

OTHER:

Our Wedding Gift Registry

STORE:

Address: **Login Username:**

Email: **Password:**

Website URL:

STORE:

Address: **Login Username:**

Email: **Password:**

Website URL:

STORE:

Address: **Login Username:**

Email: **Password:**

Website URL:

STORE:

Address: **Login Username:**

Email: **Password:**

Website URL:

OTHER:

Notes

Important Contacts

OUR WEDDING CEREMONY VENUE:

PHONE: _____   CONTACT NAME: _____

EMAIL: _____   ADDRESS: _____

OUR WEDDING PLANNER:

PHONE: _____   CONTACT NAME: _____

EMAIL: _____   ADDRESS: _____

OUR RECEPTION VENUE:

PHONE: _____   CONTACT NAME: _____

EMAIL: _____   ADDRESS: _____

OUR OFFICIANT:

PHONE: _____   CONTACT NAME: _____

EMAIL: _____   ADDRESS: _____

OUR CATERER:

PHONE: _____   CONTACT NAME: _____

EMAIL: _____   ADDRESS: _____

OUR FLORIST:

PHONE: _____   CONTACT NAME: _____

EMAIL: _____   ADDRESS: _____

Important Contacts

OUR WEDDING CAKE BAKER:

PHONE: _____ CONTACT NAME: _____

EMAIL: _____ ADDRESS: _____

THE BRIDAL SHOP(S):

PHONE: _____ CONTACT NAME: _____

EMAIL: _____ ADDRESS: _____

THE HAIR & NAIL SALON:

PHONE: _____ CONTACT NAME: _____

EMAIL: _____ ADDRESS: _____

OUR VIDEOGRAPHER:

PHONE: _____ CONTACT NAME: _____

EMAIL: _____ ADDRESS: _____

OUR PHOTOGRAPHER:

PHONE: _____ CONTACT NAME: _____

EMAIL: _____ ADDRESS: _____

OUR DJ/MUSIC:

PHONE: _____ CONTACT NAME: _____

EMAIL: _____ ADDRESS: _____

Important Contacts

MAKEUP ARTIST:

PHONE: CONTACT NAME:

EMAIL: ADDRESS:

OUR TRANSPORTATION SERVICE:

PHONE: CONTACT NAME:

EMAIL: ADDRESS:

OUR HONEYMOON ACCOMMODATIONS:

PHONE: CONTACT NAME:

EMAIL: ADDRESS:

RENTAL ITEMS (decorations, centerpieces, etc.):

PHONE: CONTACT NAME:

EMAIL: ADDRESS:

NOTES:

Notes

Wedding Planner

ENGAGEMENT PARTY:

DATE: _____   LOCATION: _____

TIME: _____   NUMBER OF GUESTS: _____

> NOTES:

BRIDAL SHOWER:

DATE: _____   LOCATION: _____

TIME: _____   NUMBER OF GUESTS: _____

> NOTES:

JACQUIE & JILL PARTY:

DATE: _____   LOCATION: _____

TIME: _____   NUMBER OF GUESTS: _____

> NOTES:

Bridal Shower Specifics

GUEST LIST:	GIFT RECEIVED FROM GUEST:	THANK YOU NOTE SENT:	
		Y	N
_____	_____	☐	☐
_____	_____	☐	☐
_____	_____	☐	☐
_____	_____	☐	☐
_____	_____	☐	☐
_____	_____	☐	☐
_____	_____	☐	☐
_____	_____	☐	☐
_____	_____	☐	☐
_____	_____	☐	☐
_____	_____	☐	☐
_____	_____	☐	☐
_____	_____	☐	☐
_____	_____	☐	☐
_____	_____	☐	☐
_____	_____	☐	☐
_____	_____	☐	☐
_____	_____	☐	☐
_____	_____	☐	☐
_____	_____	☐	☐
_____	_____	☐	☐

Bridal Shower Specifics

GUEST LIST:	GIFT RECEIVED FROM GUEST:	THANK YOU NOTE SENT: Y	N
		☐	☐
		☐	☐
		☐	☐
		☐	☐
		☐	☐
		☐	☐
		☐	☐
		☐	☐
		☐	☐
		☐	☐
		☐	☐
		☐	☐
		☐	☐
		☐	☐
		☐	☐
		☐	☐
		☐	☐
		☐	☐
		☐	☐
		☐	☐

Our Wedding Budget

USE THIS PAGE for TOTALS & A QUICK-GLANCE OVERVIEW. USE THE ITEMIZED EXPENSE TRACKERS IN THE REST OF THE BOOK FOR MORE DETAILED BREAKDOWNS.

	PROPOSED BUDGET	ACTUAL COST	DEPOSIT	REMAINDER DUE	DUE DATE
WEDDING CEREMONY VENUE					
RECEPTION VENUE					
CATERER					
FLORIST					
OFFICIANT					
WEDDING CAKE/BAKER					
BRIDE 1'S ATTIRE					
BRIDES' JEWELRY					
BRIDE 2'S ATTIRE					
BRIDESMAIDS' ATTIRE					
NAIL SALON					
HAIR					
PHOTOGRAPHER					
VIDEOGRAPHER					
DJ SERVICE/MUSIC					
INVITATIONS					
RENTALS					
WEDDING PARTY GIFTS					
TRANSPORTATION					
HONEYMOON					

Wedding Budget, continued

	PROPOSED BUDGET	ACTUAL COST	DEPOSIT	REMAINDER DUE	DUE DATE
MAKE-UP APPLICATION					
TOTAL:					

Bride 1's Attire

- [ ] WEDDING DRESS/SUIT
- [ ] SHOES
- [ ] 2ND PAIR OF COMFORTABLE SHOES FOR LATER
- [ ] NECKLACE
- [ ] EARRINGS
- [ ] ENGAGEMENT RING
- [ ] VEIL OR HEADPIECE/HAIR ACCESSORIES
- [ ] CLUTCH BAG
- [ ] JACKET OR SHRUG IN CASE IT'S COLD

- [ ] LINGERIE
- [ ] BRIDAL GARTER
- [ ] _____
- [ ] _____
- [ ] _____
- [ ] _____
- [ ] _____
- [ ] _____
- [ ] _____

OTHER THINGS TO REMEMBER:
Something old, something new, something borrowed, something blue

Bride 2's Attire

- [ ] WEDDING DRESS/SUIT
- [ ] SHOES
- [ ] 2ND PAIR OF COMFORTABLE SHOES FOR LATER
- [ ] NECKLACE
- [ ] EARRINGS
- [ ] ENGAGEMENT RING
- [ ] VEIL OR HEADPIECE/HAIR ACCESSORIES
- [ ] CLUTCH BAG
- [ ] JACKET OR SHRUG IN CASE IT'S COLD

- [ ] LINGERIE
- [ ] BRIDAL GARTER
- [ ] _____
- [ ] _____
- [ ] _____
- [ ] _____
- [ ] _____
- [ ] _____

OTHER THINGS TO REMEMBER:
Something old, something new, something borrowed, something blue

Bridal Attire Expense Tracker

ITEM PURCHASED	TOTAL COST	AMOUNT PAID	REMAINDER DUE	DUE DATE
WEDDING DRESS				
WEDDING DRESS ALTERATIONS				

Bridal Attire Expense Tracker, continued

ITEM PURCHASED	TOTAL COST	AMOUNT PAID	REMAINDER DUE	DUE DATE

12 – 15 Months Before Our Wedding

- ☐ SET THE DATE
- ☐ SET OUR OVERALL BUDGET
- ☐ CHOOSE OUR THEME (COLORS & STYLE)
- ☐ CHOOSE ENGAGEMENT PARTY
- ☐ RESEARCH VENUES
- ☐ BOOK A WEDDING PLANNER
- ☐ RESEARCH PHOTOGRAPHERS
- ☐ RESEARCH VIDEOGRAPHERS
- ☐ RESEARCH DJ'S/MUSIC

- ☐ CONSIDER FLORISTS
- ☐ RESEARCH CATERERS
- ☐ DECIDE ON OFFICIANT
- ☐ CREATE INITIAL GUEST LIST
- ☐ CHOOSE WEDDING PARTY
- ☐ SHOP FOR WEDDING DRESS
- ☐ REGISTER WITH GIFT REGISTRIES
- ☐ DISCUSS HONEYMOON IDEAS & SET BUDGET
- ☐ RESEARCH WEDDING RINGS

THINGS TO REMEMBER: TIP: *Use pages inside this book to help you with your research*

9—12 Months Before Our Wedding

- [ ] FINALIZE GUEST LIST
- [ ] ORDER INVITATIONS
- [ ] PLAN OUR RECEPTION
- [ ] BOOK PHOTOGRAPHER
- [ ] BOOK VIDEOGRAPHER
- [ ] BOOK FLORIST
- [ ] BOOK DJ/MUSIC
- [ ] BOOK CATERER
- [ ] CHOOSE WEDDING CAKE

- [ ] CHOOSE WEDDING GOWN
- [ ] ORDER WEDDING PARTY'S CLOTHING
- [ ] BOOK ROOMS FOR GUESTS
- [ ] ARRANGE & BOOK TRANSPORTATION
- [ ] BOOK WEDDING CEREMONY VENUE
- [ ] BOOK RECEPTION VENUE
- [ ] PLAN HONEYMOON
- [ ] BOOK OFFICIANT
- [ ] BOOK ROOMS FOR GUESTS

THINGS TO REMEMBER:
**TIP: Record your choices on the enclosed pages in this book under "Important Contacts" for easy access.

6 Months Before Our Wedding

- [ ] ORDER THANK YOU NOTES
- [ ] REVIEW RECEPTION DETAILS
- [ ] MAKE APPT FOR DRESS/SUIT FITTING
- [ ] CONFIRM WEDDING PARTY'S ATTIRE
- [ ] GET OUR MARRIAGE LICENSE

- [ ] BOOK HAIR STYLIST/MAKE UP ARTIST
- [ ] CONFIRM MUSIC SELECTIONS
- [ ] PLAN BRIDAL SHOWER
- [ ] PLAN WEDDING REHEARSAL
- [ ] SHOP FOR WEDDING RINGS

THINGS TO REMEMBER:
TIP: Use the Bridal Shower Guest sheet list to add names to. It is located in this book.

3 Months Before Our Wedding

- [ ] MAIL OUT INVITATIONS
- [ ] MEET WITH OFFICIANT
- [ ] BUY GIFTS FOR WEDDING PARTY
- [ ] BOOK FINAL GOWN FITTING
- [ ] BUY WEDDING BANDS
- [ ] PLAN YOUR HAIR STYLES
- [ ] PURCHASE SHOES/HEELS
- [ ] CONFIRM PASSPORTS ARE VALID

- [ ] FINALIZE RECEPTION MENU
- [ ] PLAN REHEARSAL DINNER
- [ ] CONFIRM ALL BOOKINGS
- [ ] APPLY FOR MARRIAGE LICENSE
- [ ] CONFIRM MUSIC SELECTIONS
- [ ] DRAFT WEDDING VOWS
- [ ] CHOOSE OUR MC
- [ ] ARRANGE/BOOK AIRPORT TRANSFER

THINGS TO REMEMBER:

1 Month Before Our Wedding

- ☐ CONFIRM FINAL GUEST COUNT
- ☐ CONFIRM RECEPTION DETAILS
- ☐ ATTEND FINAL GOWN/SUIT FITTING
- ☐ CONFIRM PHOTOGRAPHER
- ☐ WRAP WEDDING PARTY GIFTS
- ☐ CREATE PHOTOGRAPHY SHOT LIST

- ☐ IF MARRYING IN A CHURCH, CHOOSE READINGS
- ☐ BOOK MANI-PEDI
- ☐ CONFIRM WITH FLORIST
- ☐ CONFIRM VIDEOGRAPHER
- ☐ PICK UP WEDDING PARTY'S ATTIRE
- ☐ CREATE WEDDING SCHEDULE

THINGS TO REMEMBER:

1 Week Before Our Wedding

- [ ] FINALIZE SEATING PLANS
- [ ] MAKE PAYMENTS TO VENDORS
- [ ] PACK FOR HONEYMOON (Packing list enclosed)
- [ ] CONFIRM HOTEL RESERVATIONS
- [ ] GIVE SCHEDULE TO WEDDING PARTY

- [ ] DELIVER LICENSE TO OFFICIANT
- [ ] CONFIRM WITH BAKERY
- [ ] PICK UP WEDDING DRESS
- [ ] PICK UP WEDDING PARTY'S ATTIRE, if not done previously
- [ ] GIVE MUSIC LIST TO DJ

THINGS TO REMEMBER:

1 Week Before The Big Day

	THINGS TO DO:	NOTES:
MONDAY		
TUESDAY		
WEDNESDAY		
THURSDAY		

REMINDERS & NOTES:

1 Week Before The Big Day

	THINGS TO DO:	NOTES:
FRIDAY		
SATURDAY		
SUNDAY		

LEFT TO DO:

REMINDERS:

NOTES:

1 Day Before Our Wedding

- [ ] GET MANICURE/PEDICURE
- [ ] ATTEND REHEARSAL DINNER
- [ ]

- [ ] GIVE GIFTS TO WEDDING PARTY
- [ ] FINALIZE PACKING

TO DO LIST:

The Big Day is Here!

- [ ] GET HAIR & MAKE UP DONE
- [ ] HAVE A HEALTHY BREAKFAST
- [ ] PHOTOS

- [ ] MEET WITH WEDDING PARTY
- [ ] GIVE RINGS TO RING BEARER OR OTHER

TO DO LIST:

Our Wedding Vows

THINGS TO INCLUDE/NOT TO FORGET TO ADD:

Our Amazing Wedding Party

NAME:

PHONE: **ATTIRE SIZE:**   **SHOE SIZE:**

EMAIL:

NAME:

PHONE: **ATTIRE SIZE:**   **SHOE SIZE:**

EMAIL:

NAME:

PHONE: **ATTIRE SIZE:**   **SHOE SIZE:**

EMAIL:

NAME:

PHONE: **ATTIRE SIZE:**   **SHOE SIZE:**

EMAIL:

FLOWER GIRL / JUNIOR BRIDESMAID OR RING BEARER:

PHONE: **ATTIRE SIZE:**   **SHOE SIZE:**

EMAIL:

Notes

Choose Wedding Ceremony Venue

POSSIBLE WEDDING VENUES	PRICE OF VENUE	AVAILABLE DATES	PROS & CONS

NOTES & REMINDERS:

Tips for Choosing the Wedding Venue(s) – Ceremony & Reception

1. Start sooner than later! Popular venues book up quickly.
2. It is usually easier to choose your venue first, and then choose your wedding date based on availability of venues. Just be sure to have some ideas of particular dates that absolutely will not work for your wedding.
3. Determine if your wedding ceremony and reception will be held in two different locations or at just one location. If it will be held at two locations, as in the case of a church and then a reception hall, be sure you factor driving time into the equation. Also consider your out-of-town guests, and how easy it will be for them to find the venues. You will also want to factor in time for taking photos, if you have to drive between venues.
4. Will the venue you choose allow you to hold your wedding ceremony there too?
5. Consider the style or theme of your wedding. Will an indoor or indoor/outdoor venue fit the theme?
6. Consider the season you are getting married. If there is the potential for cool or very hot weather, will the venue you choose be comfortable for you and your guests?
7. You want to make sure that the size of the venue is appropriate. This means that there should be enough space for all your guests. In addition, don't make the mistake of renting a venue that is too large for the number of guests you will have, otherwise you may have to spend more on decorations and flowers.
8. Speaking of decorations & flowers, will the venue you choose need a lot of work (and hence more money) to get it to look like you want it to?
9. Find out if the catering is in-house or if you need to hire a separate caterer that you bring in.
10. If the catering is in-house, can you set up an appointment to discuss menus, and for taste testing before booking?
11. Before booking, make sure you know everything that is and isn't included in the fees.

Wedding Venue(s), continued

12. Are you allowed to bring in your own vendors, or is there a restriction for that particular venue? (ex. bartenders, caterers)
13. Is there sufficient parking & bathroom stalls for your guests?
14. If your wedding takes place outdoors, is there an option to go indoors if the weather doesn't cooperate, and if so, is the space adequate for your guest list?
15. A general guideline is that 10% to 15% of your budget will be spent on your choice of venue.

Wedding Ceremony Expense Tracker

ITEMS	TOTAL COST	AMOUNT PAID	REMAINDER DUE	DUE DATE
VENUE FEE				
OFFICIANT FEE				
DECORATIONS				
FLOWERS				
MARRIAGE LICENSE				
WEDDING RINGS				

Total Cost	

Expense Tracker for

_____

ITEMS	TOTAL COST	AMOUNT PAID	REMAINDER DUE	DUE DATE

Total Cost

Notes

Choose Reception Venue

POSSIBLE RECEPTION VENUES	PRICES	AVAILABILITY	PROS & CONS

NOTES & REMINDERS:

Reception Venue Expense Tracker

ITEMS	TOTAL COST	AMOUNT PAID	REMAINDER DUE	DUE DATE
VENUE FEE				
DECORATIONS				

	Total Cost

Expense Tracker for

ITEMS	TOTAL COST	AMOUNT PAID	REMAINDER DUE	DUE DATE

Total Cost

Notes

Choose Caterer

POSSIBLE CATERERS	PRICES	AVAILABILITY	PROS & CONS

NOTES & REMINDERS:

Tips for Choosing a Caterer

1. Ask your friends, family, & recently-married couples for recommendations. If you have a wedding planner, he/she may be able to offer recommendations too.
2. Find out if the wedding venue has in-house catering. If so, the venue may also offer you a list of recommended caterers to choose from. If the venue does not offer in-house catering, then does the venue allow you to bring in your choice of caterer? Does the venue also require certificates & licensing from the chosen caterer?
3. When you are choosing a caterer, it is recommended that you already have a solid idea of the number of guests you plan to have there.
4. When scheduling interviews with a potential caterer, be sure to include taste testing.
5. Taste is important, but you also have to consider what kind of service you can expect (i.e. what is their record for preparing enough food, for serving it on time, will the staff be friendly and helpful with your guests, etc.).
6. Determine your budget. This will help you determine which caterers you can afford to hire. It also helps the caterer determine the options available to fit your budget. You will need to determine if you will be having a sit-down dinner or buffet style, for example.
7. When getting an estimate, make sure to get it broken down/itemized. For example, find out what the cost is per plate or guest, does the fee include alcohol or other drinks, cost for serving, and costs of various menu items, etc.
8. Do you get charged for guest invites that don't show?
9. When are payments due?
10. Find out what options (vegan, vegetarian, gluten-free/celiac) your caterer offers for those with special diets, and if there are additional costs.

Caterer Option #1

CONTACT INFORMATION:

PHONE: ....

CONTACT NAME: ....

EMAIL: ....

ADDRESS: ....

MENU CHOICE #1:

MENU CHOICE #2:

	YES ✓	NO ✓	COST:
BAR INCLUDED:	☐	☐	....
CORKAGE FEE:	☐	☐	....
HORS D'OEUVRES:	☐	☐	....
TAXES INCLUDED:	☐	☐	....
GRATUITIES INCLUDED:	☐	☐	

Menu Planner

TIP: Be sure to include gluten-free and vegetarian or vegan options for your guests

HORS D'OEUVRES

1st COURSE:

2nd COURSE:

3rd COURSE:

4th COURSE:

DESSERT:

Caterer Option #2

CONTACT INFORMATION:

PHONE: _____   CONTACT NAME: _____

EMAIL: _____   ADDRESS: _____

MENU CHOICE #1:

MENU CHOICE #2:

	YES ✓	NO ✓	COST:
BAR INCLUDED:	☐	☐	
CORKAGE FEE:	☐	☐	
HORS D'OEUVRES:	☐	☐	
TAXES INCLUDED:	☐	☐	
GRATUITIES INCLUDED:	☐	☐	

Menu Planner

TIP: Be sure to include gluten-free and vegetarian or vegan options for your guests

HORS D'OEUVRES

1st COURSE:

2nd COURSE:

3rd COURSE:

4th COURSE:

DESSERT:

Notes

Caterer Expense Tracker

ITEMS	TOTAL COST	AMOUNT PAID	REMAINDER DUE	DUE DATE
CATERING/FOOD				
WEDDING CAKE				

Total Cost

Notes

Wedding Cake

PHONE: _____   COMPANY: _____

EMAIL: _____   ADDRESS: _____

WEDDING CAKE PACKAGE:

COST: _____   FREE TASTING: _____   DELIVERY FEE: _____

FLAVOR: _____

FILLING: _____

SIZE: _____

SHAPE: _____

COLOR: _____

EXTRAS: _____

TOTAL COST:

NOTES:

Notes

Choose Videographer

POSSIBLE VIDEOGRAPHERS	PRICES	AVAILABILITY	PROS/CONS

NOTES & REMINDERS:

Tips for Choosing a Videographer

1. You should ask your photographer if he knows of any videographers that he can recommend. You want to know that your chosen photographer and videographer will work well together to capture the special moments of your big day. Also be sure to ask family & recently-married friends for suggestions.

2. Find a videographer that is familiar with filming in the type of setting that you will be getting married (i.e. indoors vs. outdoors).

3. Consider whether you want your final video to be more of a chronological documentary, or more of a cinematic nature. Also determine what parts of the day you want filmed, and if there are any parts of the day that you don't want filmed (and if the price varies). Some couples like to be interviewed separately or together before their wedding too, so consider if that's something your videographer would do for you.

4. Then ask the videographer to allow you to see several wedding videos that he has done so that you can get a feel for his style and edited versions. You also want to pay attention to the lighting and the audio. It is a big red flag if he is not willing to share his work with you.

5. Be sure that your videographer allows your input, and gives you the opportunity to tell him what aspects of other videos, that he has done, that you liked and would like to include for your wedding too.

6. Find out how many hours of videographer time you get, and if there are discounts for less time. Also find out if there are overtime rates. You'll want to consider how driving time between venues will cut into filming.

7. You also want to hire a videographer who is willing to scout out the venue before the wedding day so that he will be fully prepared and organized.

8. Another important aspect is ensuring that the person you are talking to is the ACTUAL videographer who will be filming your day. This is especially important, when you are dealing with a business that has more than one videographer working for it.

Videographer, continued

9. Be sure to read the contract details. You'll also want to find out how long it takes to get your video back after the wedding.
10. Find out what happens if the videographer is sick on the day of your wedding. Who will cover then? Can you meet this person ahead of time?

Notes

Our Videographer Choice

VIDEOGRAPHER:

PHONE: .... COMPANY: ....

EMAIL: .... ADDRESS: ....
....

WEDDING PACKAGE OVERVIEW:

EST PRICE: ....

INCLUSIONS:	YES ✓	NO ✓	COST:
DUPLICATES/COPIES:	☐	☐	
PHOTO MONTAGE:	☐	☐	
MUSIC ADDED:	☐	☐	
EDITING:	☐	☐	

TOTAL COST:

NOTES:

Choose Photographer

POSSIBLE PHOTOGRAPHERS	PRICES	AVAILABILITY	WHAT IS & ISN'T INCLUDED IN PHOTO PACKAGE, PROS/CONS

NOTES & REMINDERS:

Photographer Option #1

PHOTOGRAPHER:

PHONE: _____ **COMPANY:** _____

EMAIL: _____ **ADDRESS:** _____

_____

WEDDING PACKAGE OVERVIEW:

EST PRICE: _____

INCLUSIONS:	YES ✓	NO ✓	COST:
ENGAGEMENT SHOOT:	☐	☐	
PHOTO ALBUMS:	☐	☐	
FRAMES:	☐	☐	
PROOFS INCLUDED:	☐	☐	
NEGATIVES INCLUDED:	☐	☐	

TOTAL COST:

Photographer Option #2

PHOTOGRAPHER:

PHONE: _____   **COMPANY:** _____

EMAIL: _____   **ADDRESS:** _____
                                            _____

WEDDING PACKAGE OVERVIEW:

EST PRICE: _____

INCLUSIONS:	YES ✓	NO ✓	COST:
ENGAGEMENT SHOOT:	☐	☐	
PHOTO ALBUMS:	☐	☐	
FRAMES:	☐	☐	
PROOFS INCLUDED:	☐	☐	
NEGATIVES INCLUDED:	☐	☐	

TOTAL COST:

Notes

Tips for Choosing a Photographer

1. As usual, ask friends & family for recommendations. Look at your friend's wedding albums and photos. It is preferable not to look at only a few photos, but to look at the whole day that the photographer has captured, as that will give you an idea of the overall quality of work.

2. Be sure to set a budget, and stick to it. Know what is your upper limit.

3. When considering photographers, start by looking at their personal portfolios or galleries found on websites. However, remember that the portfolios you are looking at have been carefully hand picked and chosen from the best of the best.

4. Consider the photographer's style, and whether it suits yours. Create a list of your top three to five favorite photographers.

5. If you will be taking outdoor photos, be sure to view photos that the photographer has done outdoors. You want to make sure that the photos are not washed out from the sun. In contrast, if you will be doing photos indoors, how do other indoor photos look? Are they too dark, or is there adequate lighting?

6. Meet with your list of favorite photographers. Be sure to look at full albums of all parts of a wedding, not just parts of one. You want to see if the photographer is able to capture the emotions of the day, and the elements you wish for in a photographer.

7. When you meet with a photographer, determine if your personality and that of the photographer will work well together. This is important because your photographer will be spending the whole day with you, so you want to make sure that you will get along.

8. Determine what size of party the photographer is used to photographing. For example, if you plan for some photos of 20 people or those including children with the bride and groom, can the photographer demonstrate nice photos of groups of this size or with children?

9. Find out what is included in different photography packages, and how much they cost. For example, does the photographer's photo package include 8 hours of service? Does the price change if you need the photographer for less or more time? Does the price include a CD or a completed album, etc.? Do you even need to buy a package or can you buy a-la-carte photos? Can you get a discount if you leave certain parts out of the package (i.e. parent albums)? Are engagement photos extra? Does the photographer charge mileage/travel fees, or is travel time included in the day and price? Does it cost more for retouching or special effects? Don't assume anything. Be straightforward with what you want, and see what options the photographer can provide.

10. Read the photography contract. Find out how long it takes to get the images back. If the photographer owns the rights to the images, are you only able to post watermarked ones online? Does the photographer plan to post images from your wedding on his/her website and in portfolio albums for promotional purposes? Are you allowed to print the photos yourself, or do you need to order them from the photographer?

11. If there are particular shots you want, be sure to let the photographer know this ahead of time. However, don't try to micromanage the photographer. This will only take away from the photographer's concentration and attention during the wedding day.

12. Find out if there is a need for more than one photographer to be shooting on the day of the wedding. This can be useful for large weddings. However, it can also come with additional costs so you need to determine what exactly you want and you can realistically afford.

Expense Tracker for Photographer

ITEMS	TOTAL COST	AMOUNT PAID	REMAINDER DUE	DUE DATE

Total Cost

Choose DJ/Music

POSSIBLE DJ's & MUSIC & PHONE No.	PRICES	AVAILABILITY (Dates & Times)	PROS & CONS

NOTES & REMINDERS:

Expense Tracker for DJ/Music

ITEMS	TOTAL COST	AMOUNT PAID	REMAINDER DUE	DUE DATE

Total Cost

Tips for Choosing a DJ

1. Ask recently-married friends and family for recommendations. In particular, you are looking for DJ's who are experienced with weddings.

2. Is it a professional, long-time business with good reviews, or is it a kid trying to make extra money on weekends? Obviously, you want to choose the former.

3. Some DJ businesses may have more than one DJ. Make sure you can meet with them, and choose the one that you want to work with at your wedding. Also find out what happens if that particular DJ is sick on the day of your wedding.

4. Consider the personality of the DJ. Does the DJ know how to work a crowd, and get the guests on the dance floor? Does the DJ understand the progression of a wedding (i.e. bride's and groom's first dance, father-daughter dance, etc.)? Does the DJ know how to cater the music to the various ages attending the wedding?

5. Does the DJ do a visit at your chosen venues to ensure the acoustics are right, and that he will be able to fit all his equipment at the venues? If not, then that DJ is probably not a good fit for you.

6. Does the DJ have back-up equipment available ON SITE if something goes wrong?

7. Is there any extra equipment (i.e. tables) that you need to rent? Do you need to provide tablecloths so that the guests don't see a bunch of wires?

8. How well does the DJ blend or transition the music from one song to the next?

9. Find out what other options exist and their cost – for example, special lighting.

10. Are you allowed to provide a playlist and a "do not play" list? Ensure the DJ has a good understanding of the genre of music you want.

11. Be very careful about allowing karaoke, unless you don't mind listening to people who can't sing well, and decide to monopolize the microphone.

12. You will want to choose a DJ that does not play the music so loud that the guests who are not on the dancefloor cannot have a conversation with one another.

13. Find out what time the DJ arrives to set up his equipment at the venue.

DJ, Continued

14. Find out if the DJ will be the one (if you choose that) announcing your first dance, the throwing of the bouquet, etc.? Decide all of this ahead of time, as some DJ's may not do this, and therefore you will need to determine if your maid of honor or someone else will have this duty or not. Will the DJ allow you to provide an itinerary (ahead of time) of how you expect the night and music to progress?

15. Find out what the DJ's hours of service are. Does he charge for overtime, or is he booked elsewhere after your wedding ends?

16. Find out if the DJ has liability insurance. You'd hate for there to an equipment malfunction that causes a fire, and there is no coverage. The likelihood of that happening is small, but you need to be protected. Find our from your venue if this is required.

17. Lastly, be sure to look over the contract carefully. Look for extra hidden fees, and ask for clarification if there is anything you don't understand.

Our DJ/Music Choice

DJ/LIVE BAND/ENTERTAINMENT:

PHONE: _____   COMPANY: _____

EMAIL: _____   ADDRESS: _____

START TIME: _____   END TIME: _____

RECORD OUR SONGS FOR CEREMONY, RECEPTION, FIRST DANCE, FATHER-BRIDE DANCE, ETC.:

EST PRICE: _____

INCLUSIONS:	YES ✓	NO ✓	COST:
SOUND EQUIPMENT:	☐	☐	
LIGHTING:	☐	☐	
SPECIAL EFFECTS:	☐	☐	
GRATUITIES	☐	☐	

TOTAL COST:

NOTES:

Notes

Choose Florist

POSSIBLE FLORISTS	COSTS & WHAT IS INCLUDED	OTHER THOUGHTS

NOTES & REMINDERS:

Florist Option #1

FLORIST:

PHONE: _____ COMPANY: _____

EMAIL: _____ ADDRESS: _____

FLORAL PACKAGE:

EST PRICE: _____

INCLUSIONS:	YES ✓	NO ✓	COST:
BRIDAL BOUQUET:	☐	☐	
THROW-AWAY BOUQUET:	☐	☐	
CORSAGES:	☐	☐	
CEREMONY FLOWERS	☐	☐	
CENTERPIECES	☐	☐	
CAKE TOPPER	☐	☐	
BOUTONNIERE	☐	☐	

TOTAL COST:

Florist Option #2

FLORIST:

PHONE: .... COMPANY: ....

EMAIL: .... ADDRESS: ....

FLORAL PACKAGE:

EST PRICE: _____

INCLUSIONS:	YES ✓	NO ✓	COST:
BRIDAL BOUQUET:	☐	☐	
THROW-AWAY BOUQUET:	☐	☐	
CORSAGES:	☐	☐	
CEREMONY FLOWERS	☐	☐	
CENTERPIECES	☐	☐	
CAKE TOPPER	☐	☐	
BOUTONNIERE	☐	☐	

TOTAL COST:

Tips for Choosing a Florist

1. Set a budget . Keep reading below for more ideas that will help you set it.
2. Use Pinterest & Instagram to find pictures of flowers, bouquets, & arrangements that you like. On Instagram, use the hashtag #weddingflowers to help you.
3. Ask your friends for recommendations of which florist they used & their impressions. Look up "Reviews" of local florists online.
4. Keep your color theme in mind. When meeting with your florist, bring fabric swatches of the colors. Also, bring pictures of the styles. This can help the florist to understand if you are looking for a minimalist or elaborate approach.
5. You also want to keep the theme of your wedding in mind. For example, if you will be having an outdoor wedding in the country, you may want daisies and other wildflowers that bring your theme together.
6. Look at website photo galleries of local florist vendors to get an idea of the type of work that they do. This is because some florists specialize in smaller flower arrangements, and others in large, tall ones. If there is a particular bouquet or arrangement that you like, be sure to take note of it so that you can mention it to the florist.
7. Consider what you need the florist to do. Do you need the florist to make the floral bouquets and arrangements only, or do you need them to provide hands-on assistance with setting things up? If so, then you will need to consider this in your budget. This may also depend on whether you have a wedding planner, and what services she is providing.
8. Ask the florist which flowers are in season for the time you will be getting married. This is because certain flowers can be more expensive when they are not in season.
9. You don't have to choose the first florist you meet with! Be sure to pick your top three, based on recommendations from friends and families and photos you've seen. Then set up a time to meet with the florists to discuss your needs. You'll get a feeling whether each florist understands your needs. You should also ask for an estimate from each florist you meet with.
10. Consider starting with your bridal bouquet, and then choosing the other flower bouquets and arrangements to complement your bouquet.

Notes

Expense Tracker for Florist

ITEMS	TOTAL COST	AMOUNT PAID	REMAINDER DUE	DUE DATE

Total Cost

Bachelorette Party Planner

DATE : _____

TIME: _____

LOCATION: _____

OTHER DETAILS: _____

_____

_____

_____

TIMELINE OF EVENTS

TIME	ACTIVITY PLANNED

GUEST LIST:

_____

_____

_____

_____

_____

_____

SHOPPING LIST:

- [ ] _____
- [ ] _____
- [ ] _____
- [ ] _____
- [ ] _____
- [ ] _____
- [ ] _____
- [ ] _____

Notes

Transportation Planner

TO CEREMONY	PICK UP TIME:	PICK UP LOCATION:
BRIDE 1:		
BRIDE 2:		
BRIDE 1'S PARENTS:		
BRIDE 2'S PARENTS:		
WEDDING PARTY:		

NOTES:

TO RECEPTION:	PICK UP TIME:	PICK UP LOCATION:
BRIDE & BRIDE:		
BRIDE 1'S PARENTS:		
BRIDE 2'S PARENTS:		
WEDDING PARTY:		

Expense Tracker for

ITEMS	TOTAL COST	AMOUNT PAID	REMAINDER DUE	DUE DATE

Total Cost

Wedding Rehearsal

CEREMONY REHEARSAL:

DATE: _____   ADDRESS: _____

TIME: _____   NUMBER OF GUESTS: _____

REHEARSAL DINNER:

DATE: _____   ADDRESS: _____

TIME: _____   NUMBER OF GUESTS: _____

NOTES & REMINDERS:

Notes

Honeymoon Packing Checklist

CLOTHING

- Swimwear
- T-shirts/Tank Tops
- Underwear & Socks
- Pants
- Shorts
- Hat
- Sleepwear
- Jacket/coat
- Footwear
-
-
-

MISCELLANEOUS

- Immunization Records
-
-
-

TOILETRIES

- Toothbrush & Toothpaste
- Skin Care Products/Cosmetics
- Shampoo/Conditioner
- Hair Styling Products
- Shaver
- Soap/Body Wash
- Brush/Comb
- Female Sanitary Products
-

ELECTRONICS

- Cell phone
- Tablet & stylus
- Laptop & mouse
- Ear Buds
- Camera
- Chargers

DOCUMENTS

- Passport
- Driver's License
- Credit Cards/Bank Cards
- Airplane Tickets
- Health Card
- Insurance Documents

MEDICINE CABINET

- Contact Lenses & Contact Solution
- Eyeglasses/Sunglasses
- Vitamins & Supplements
- Tylenol, Advil, Aleve
- Prescription medications
- Cold & Sinus Medication
- Lip Balm
- Bug Spray
- Sunscreen

Honeymoon Expense Tracker

ITEM	TOTAL COST	AMOUNT PAID	REMAINDER DUE	DUE DATE
AIRLINE TICKETS				

Total Cost

Notes

Miscellanous Expense Tracker

ITEM PURCHASED/RENTED	TOTAL COST	AMOUNT PAID	REMAINDER DUE	DUE DATE

Total Cost

Expense Tracker for _____

ITEM PURCHASED/RENTED	TOTAL COST	AMOUNT PAID	REMAINDER DUE	DUE DATE

Total Cost

Expense Tracker for _____

ITEM PURCHASED/RENTED	TOTAL COST	AMOUNT PAID	REMAINDER DUE	DUE DATE

Total Cost

Wedding Guest List

**NOTE: FOR EASY CALCULATIONS, THERE ARE 20 GUESTS/PAGE

NAME:	ADDRESS:	# IN PARTY:	RSVP: ✓

Wedding Guest List

NAME:	ADDRESS:	# IN PARTY:	RSVP: ✓

Wedding Guest list

NAME:	ADDRESS:	# IN PARTY:	RSVP: ✓

Wedding Guest list

NAME:	ADDRESS:	# IN PARTY:	RSVP: ✓

Wedding Guest List

NAME:	ADDRESS:	# IN PARTY:	RSVP: ✓

Wedding Guest List

NAME:	ADDRESS:	# IN PARTY:	RSVP: ✓

Wedding Guest list

NAME:	ADDRESS:	# IN PARTY:	RSVP: ✓

Wedding Guest list

NAME:	ADDRESS:	# IN PARTY:	RSVP: ✓

Wedding Guest list

NAME:	ADDRESS:	# IN PARTY:	RSVP: ✓

Wedding Guest list

NAME:	ADDRESS:	#IN PARTY:	RSVP: ✓

Wedding Guest list

NAME:	ADDRESS:	# IN PARTY:	RSVP: ✓

Wedding Guest list

NAME:	ADDRESS:	# IN PARTY:	RSVP: ✓

Wedding Guest List

NAME:	ADDRESS:	# IN PARTY:	RSVP: ✓

Wedding Guest list

NAME:	ADDRESS:	# IN PARTY:	RSVP: ✓

Wedding Guest List

NAME:	ADDRESS:	# IN PARTY:	RSVP: ✓

Wedding Guest list

NAME:	ADDRESS:	# IN PARTY:	RSVP: ✓

Wedding Guest list

NAME:	ADDRESS:	# IN PARTY:	RSVP: ✓

Wedding Guest list

NAME:	ADDRESS:	# IN PARTY:	RSVP: ✓

Wedding Guest List

NAME:	ADDRESS:	# IN PARTY:	RSVP: ✓

Wedding Guest list

NAME:	ADDRESS:	# IN PARTY:	RSVP: ✓

Table Seating

Table #

Table #

Table #

Table #

SEATING PLANNER NOTES:

Table Seating

Table #

Table #

Table #

Table #

SEATING PLANNER NOTES:

Table Seating

Table #

Table #

Table #

Table #

SEATING PLANNER NOTES:

Table Seating

Table #

Table #

Table #

Table #

SEATING PLANNER NOTES:

Table Seating

Table #

Table #

Table #

Table #

SEATING PLANNER NOTES:

Table Seating

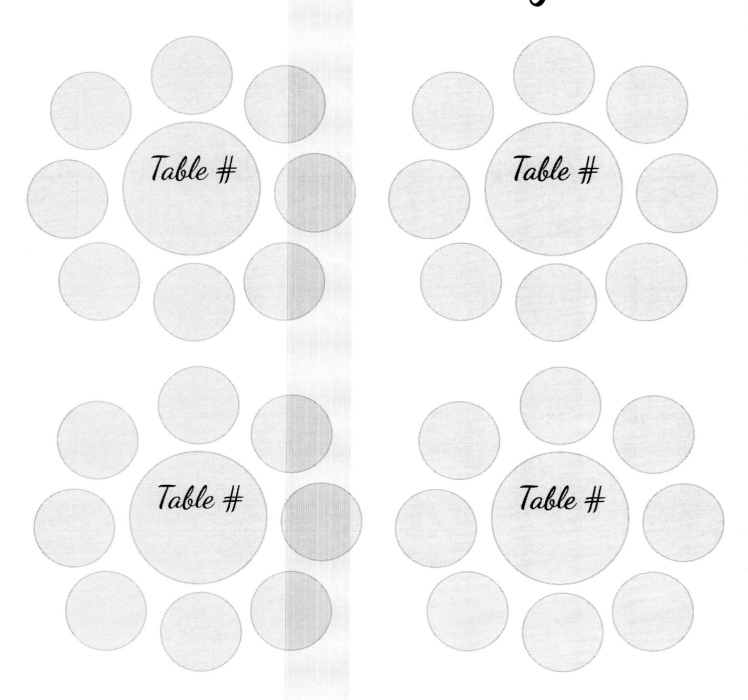

Table #

Table #

Table #

Table #

SEATING PLANNER NOTES:

Table Seating

Table #

Table #

Table #

Table #

SEATING PLANNER NOTES:

Table Seating

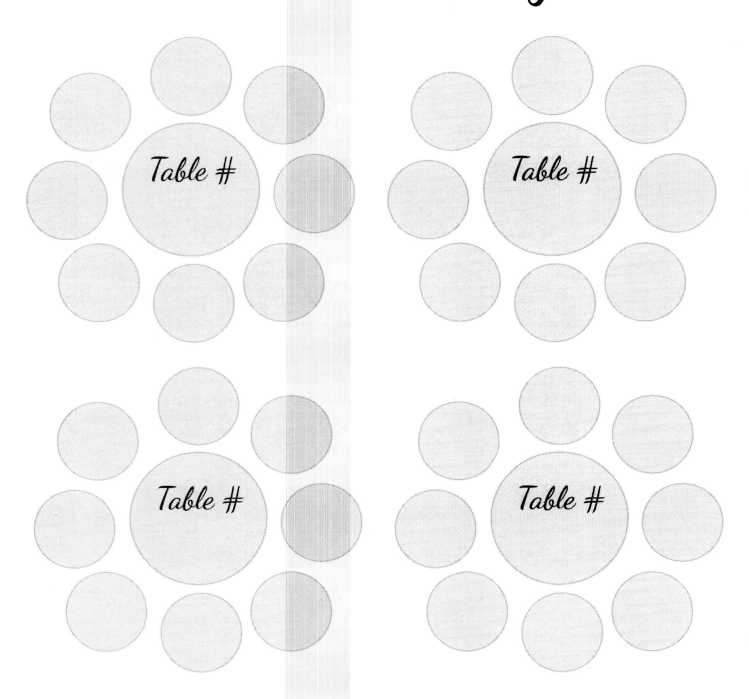

Table #

Table #

Table #

Table #

SEATING PLANNER NOTES:

Table Seating

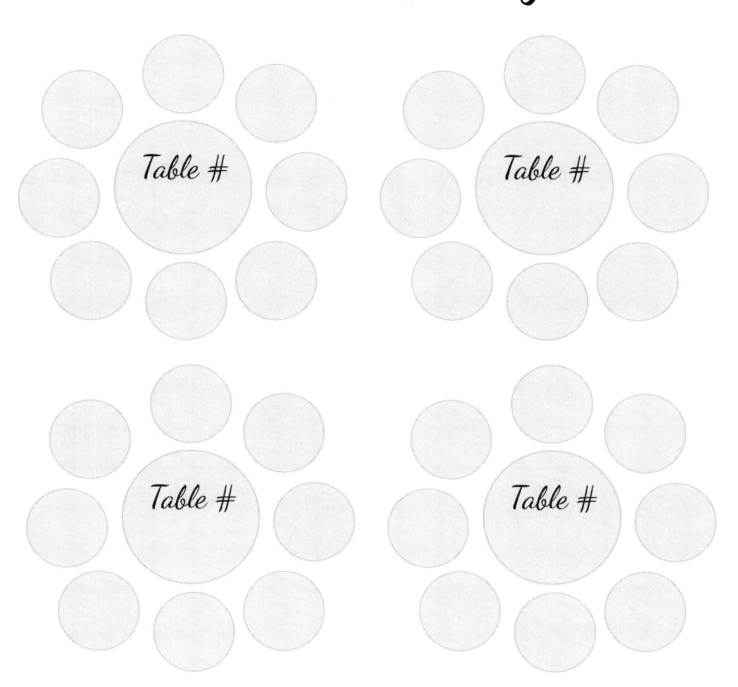

Table #

Table #

Table #

Table #

SEATING PLANNER NOTES:

Table Seating

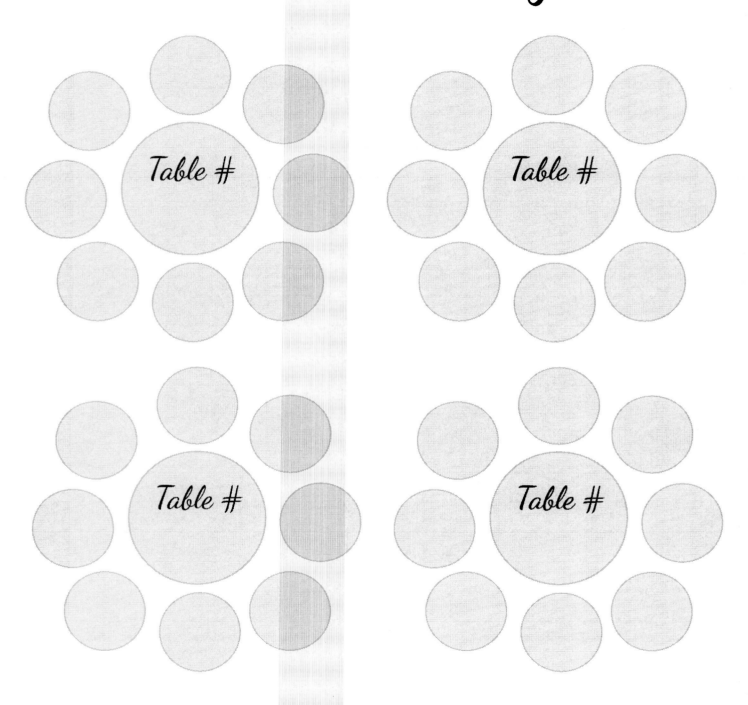

Table #

Table #

Table #

Table #

SEATING PLANNER NOTES:

Table Seating

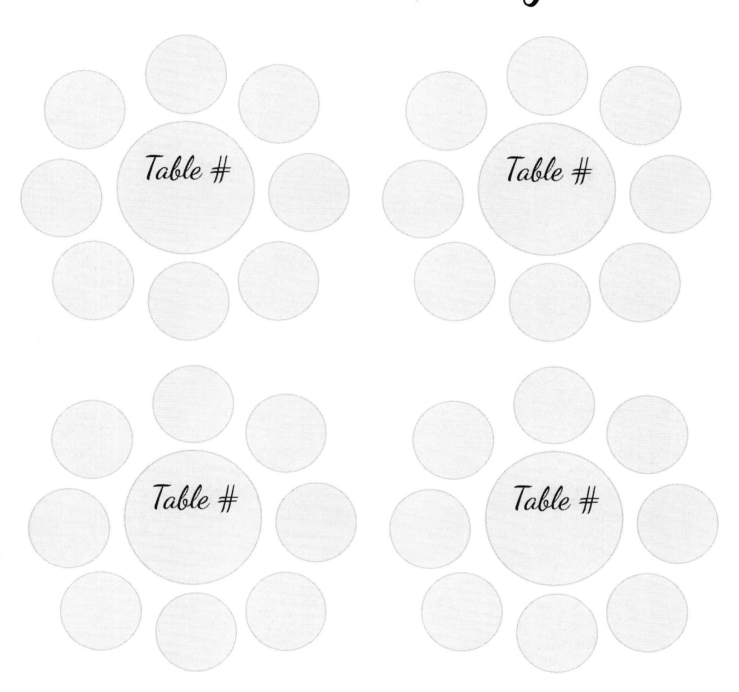

Table #

Table #

Table #

Table #

SEATING PLANNER NOTES:

Table Seating

Table #

Table #

Table #

Table #

SEATING PLANNER NOTES:

Table Seating

Table #

Table #

Table #

Table #

SEATING PLANNER NOTES:

Alternate Table Seating Planners

NOTE: In the following pages, we have included additional table seating plans that you may prefer to use for planning, depending on table shape & size. You are permitted to photocopy these seating plans for your own personal use if there are not enough of them to plan your guest's seating.

Table Seating

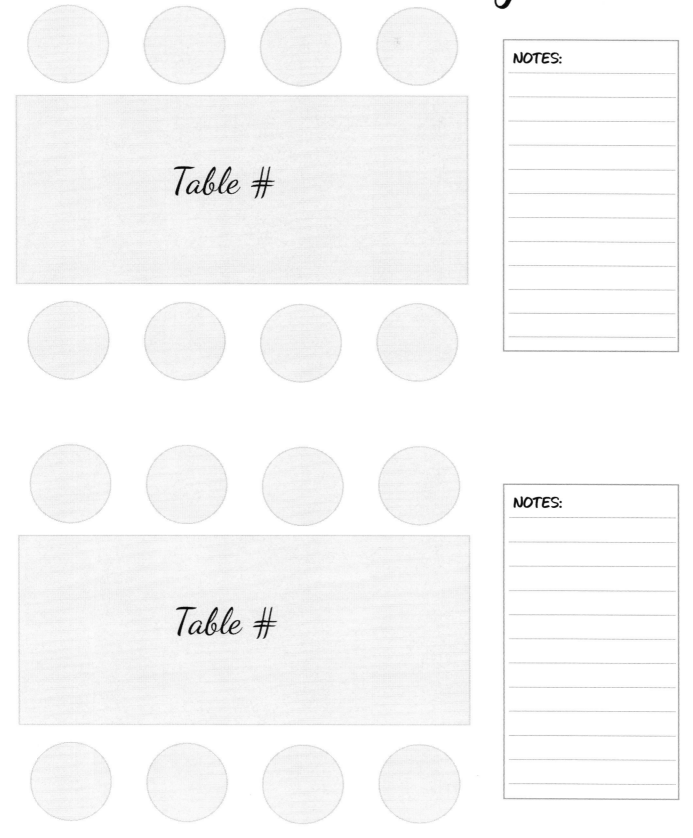

Table #

NOTES:

Table #

NOTES:

Table Seating

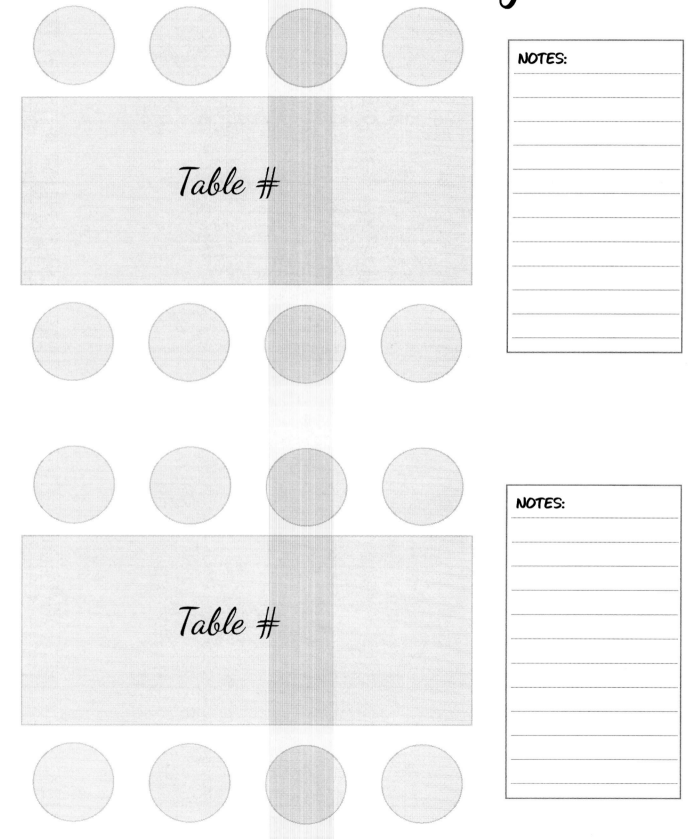

Table #

NOTES:

Table #

NOTES:

Table Seating

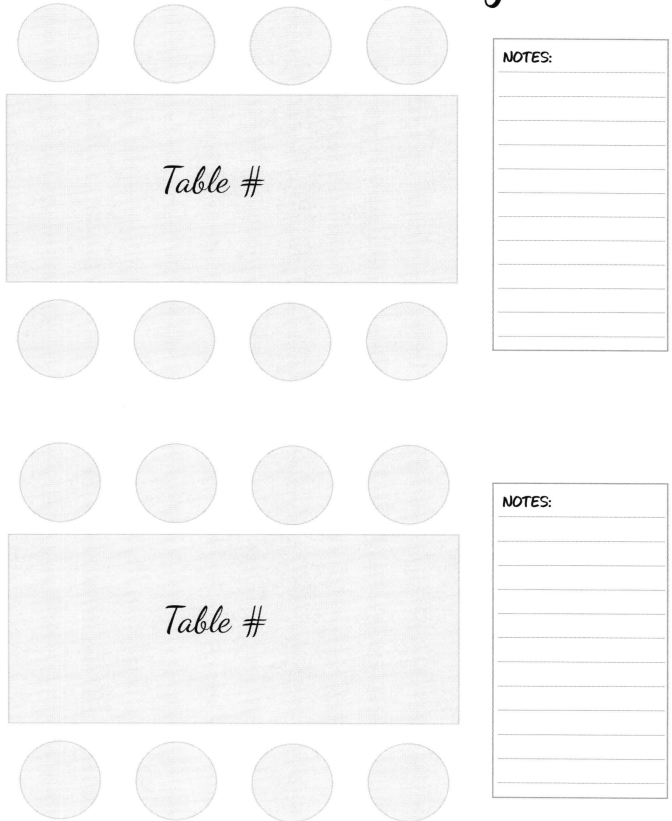

Table #

NOTES:

Table #

NOTES:

Table Seating

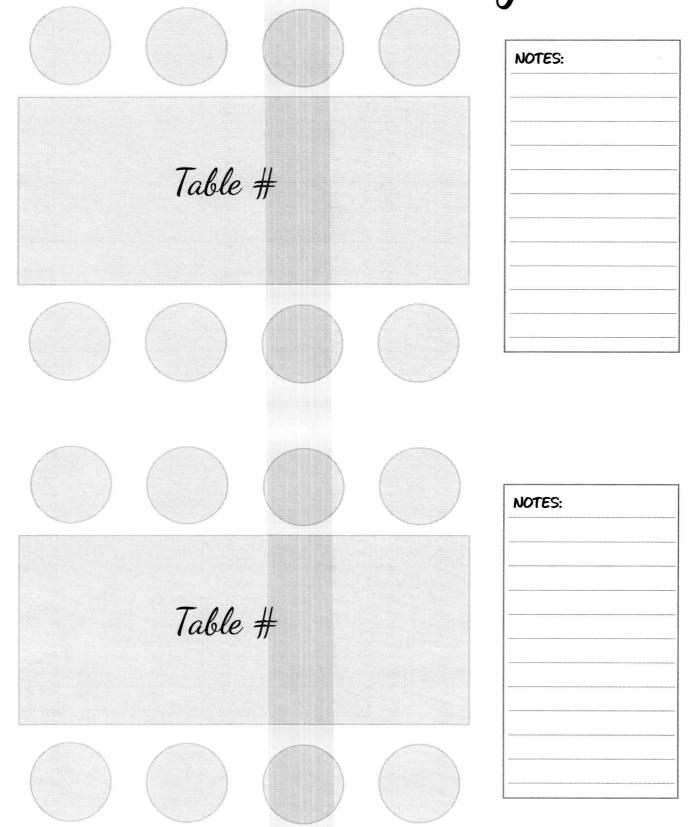

Table #

NOTES:

Table #

NOTES:

Table Seating

Table #

NOTES:

Table #

NOTES:

Table Seating

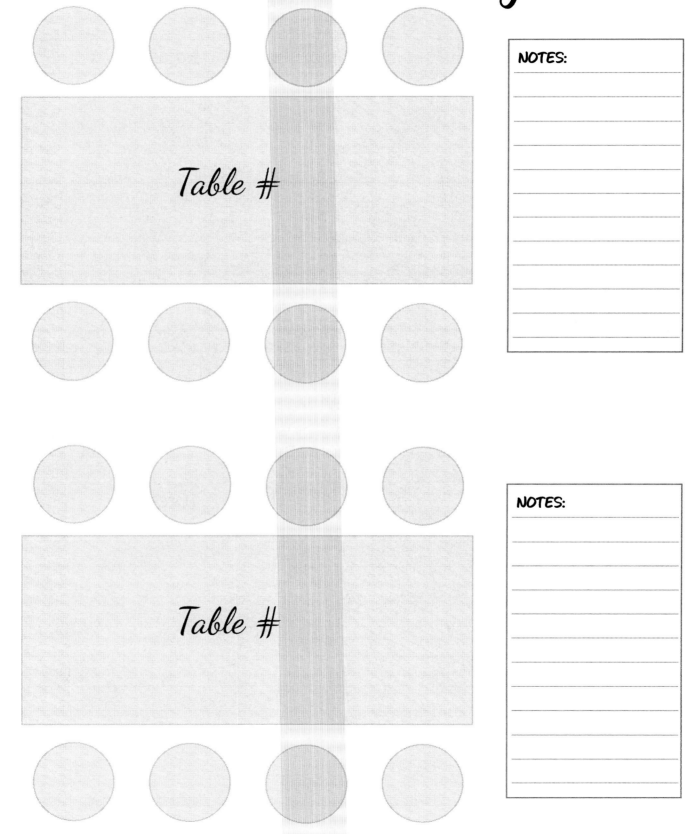

NOTES:

Table #

NOTES:

Table #

Table Seating

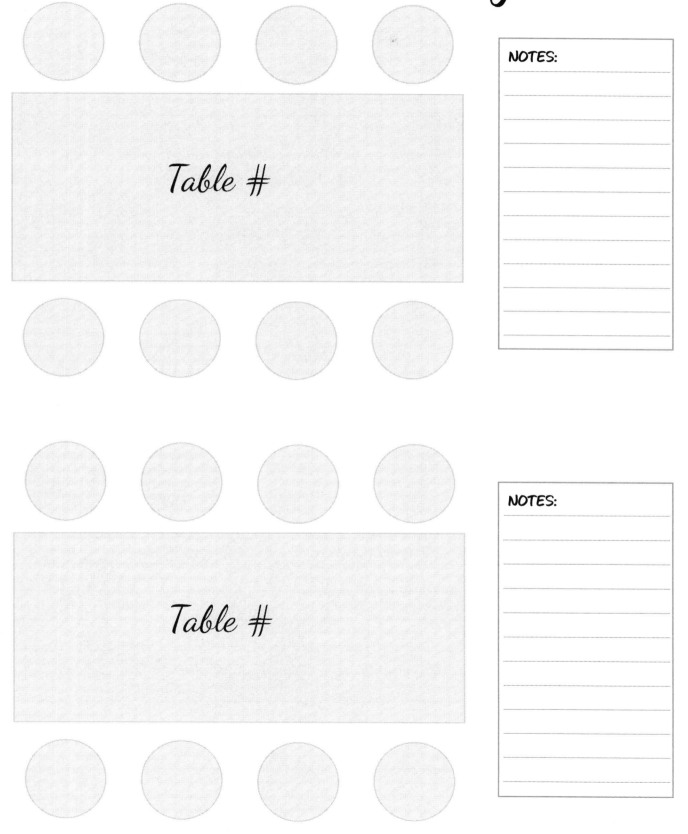

Table #

NOTES:

Table #

NOTES:

Table Seating

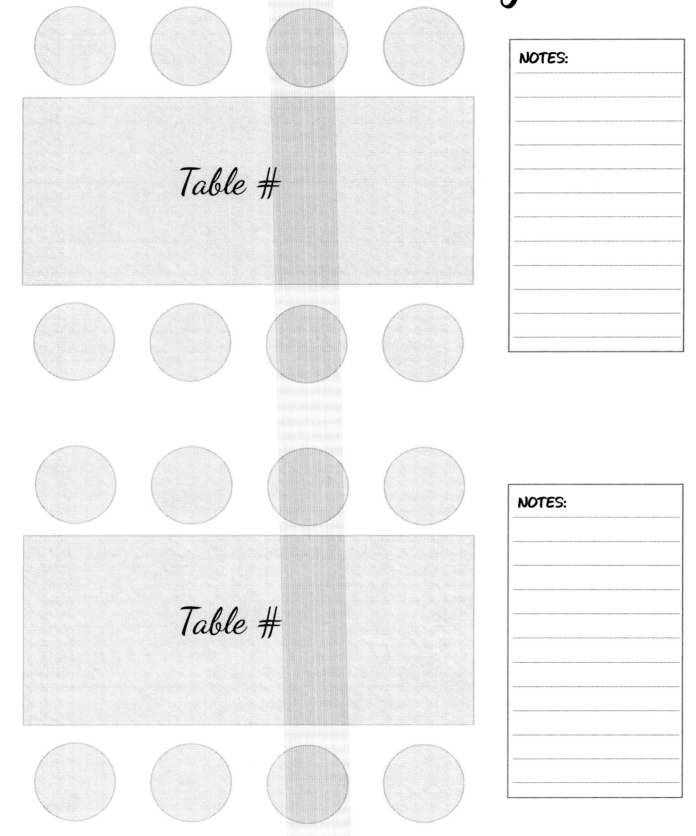

Table #

NOTES:

Table #

NOTES:

Table Seating

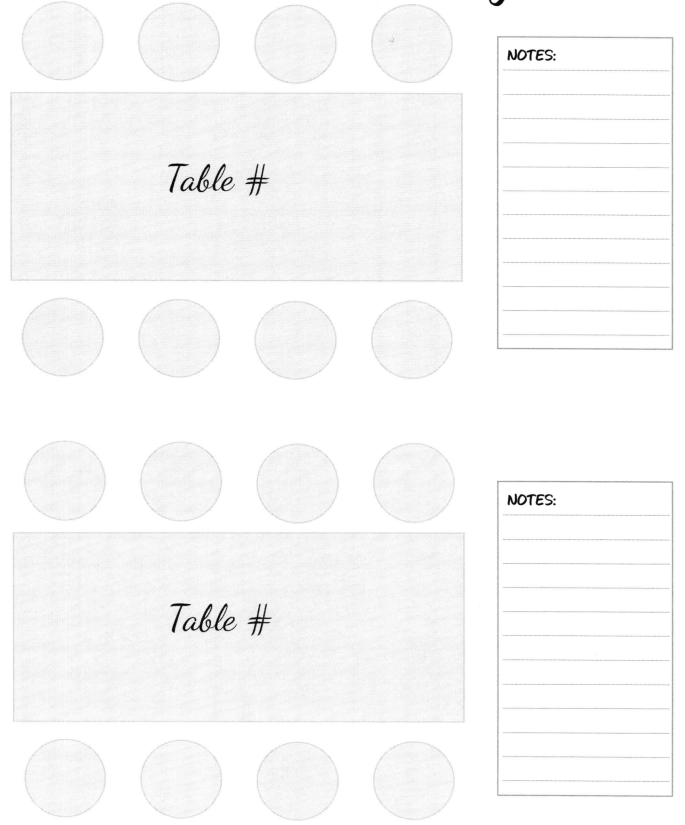

NOTES:

Table #

NOTES:

Table #

Table Seating

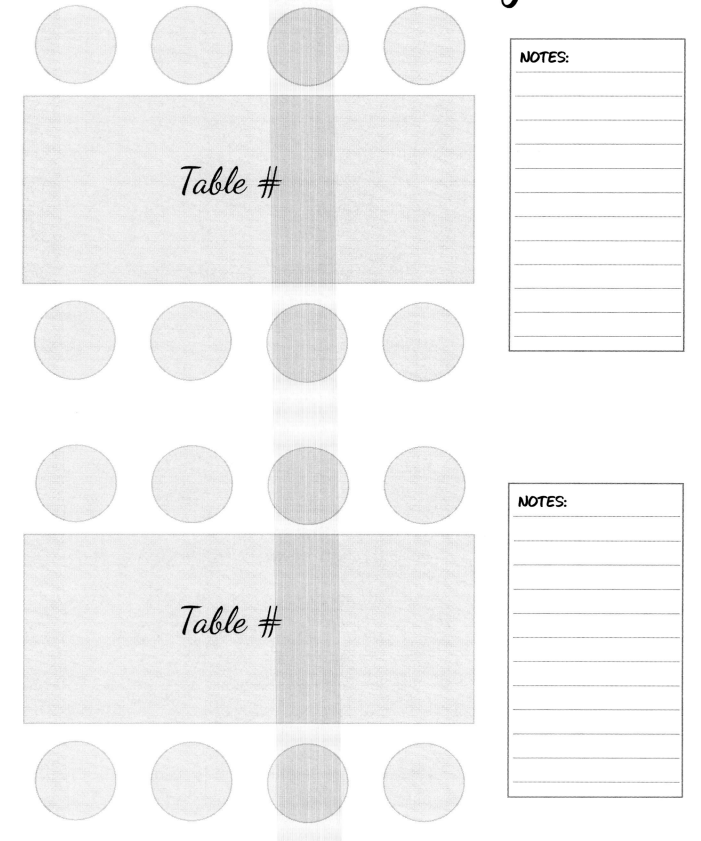

Table #

NOTES:

Table #

NOTES:

Table Seating

TABLE #

TABLE #

TABLE #

TABLE #

TABLE #

TABLE #

TABLE #

TABLE #

TABLE #

Table Seating

TABLE #

TABLE #

TABLE #

TABLE #

TABLE #

TABLE #

TABLE #

TABLE #

TABLE #

Table Seating

TABLE #

TABLE #

TABLE #

TABLE #

TABLE #

TABLE #

TABLE #

TABLE #

TABLE #

Table Seating

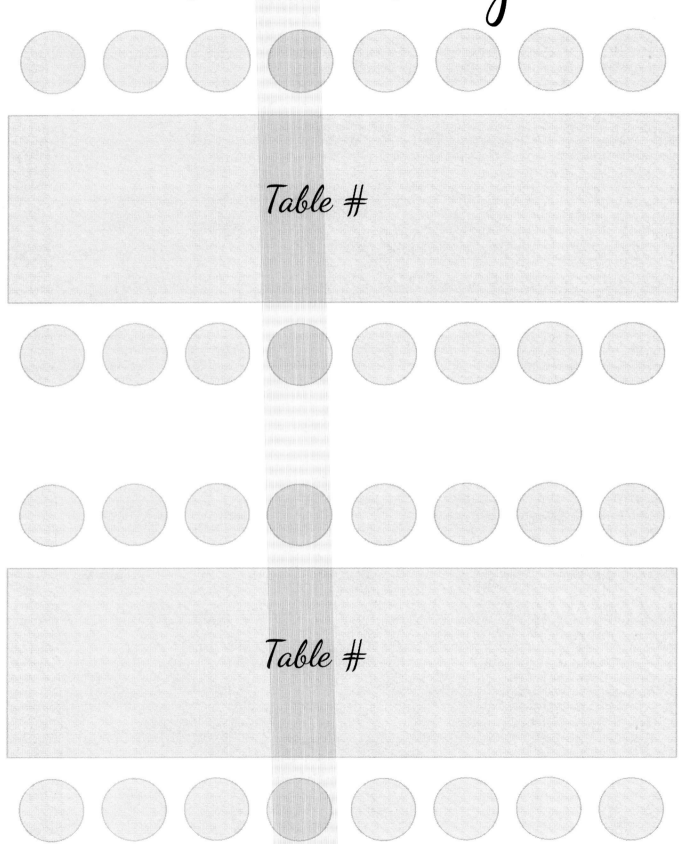

Table #

Table #

Table Seating

Table #

Table #

Table Seating

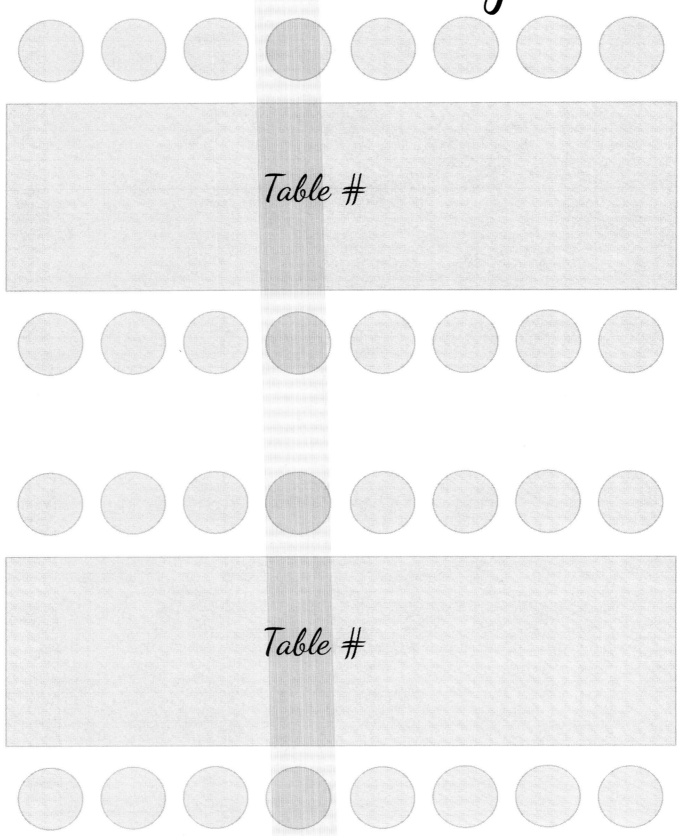

Table #

Table #

Table Seating

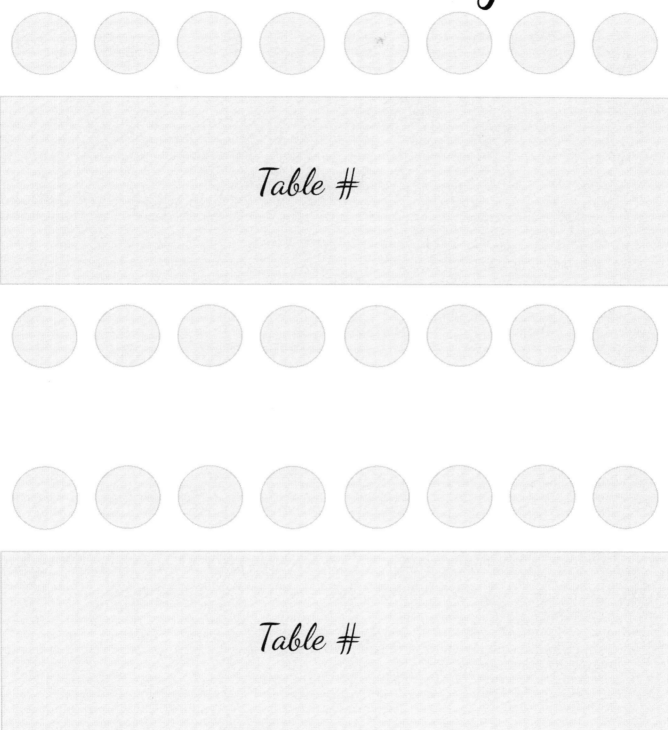

Table #

Table #

Table Seating

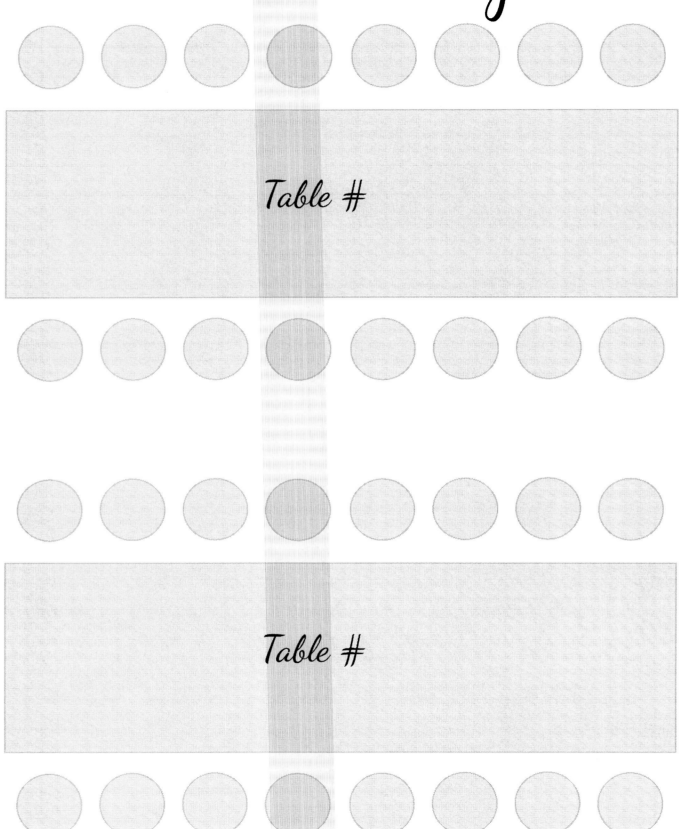

Table #

Table #

Table Seating

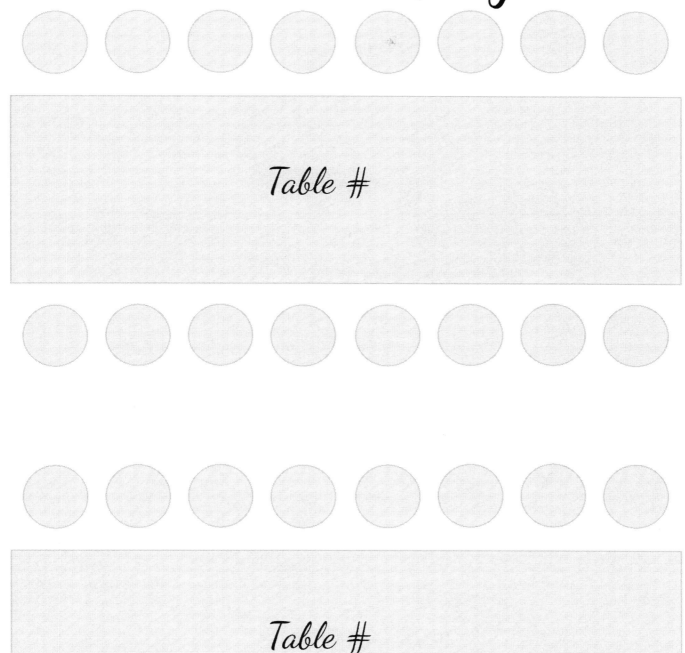

Table #

Table #

Table Seating

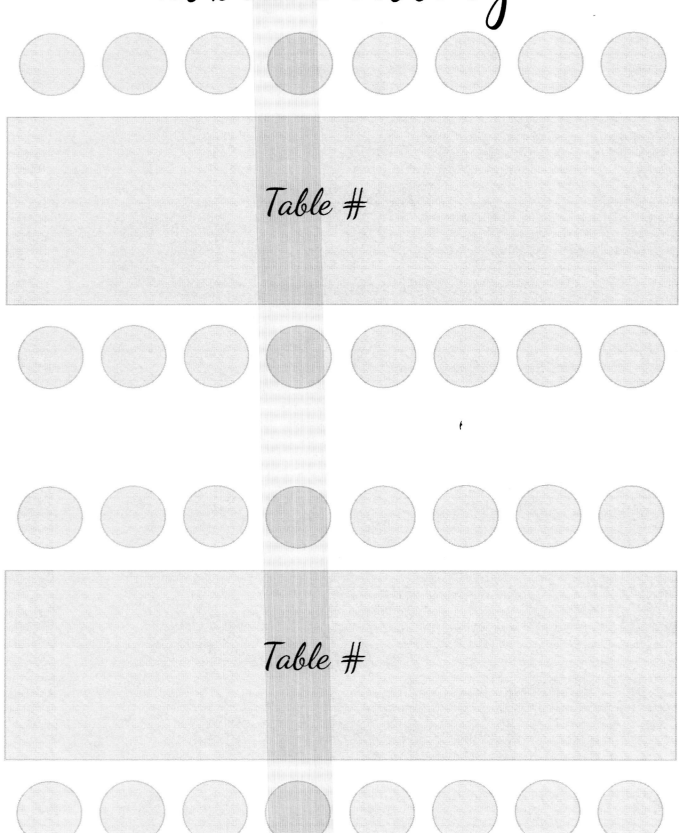

Table #

Table #

Table Seating

Table #

Table #

Notes

Notes

Notes

Just Married

Notes

Notes

Made in the USA
San Bernardino, CA
19 December 2019